The Fun Puns

Archaeologist:
A man whose career
lies in ruins.

What's the
definition of
a will?
A dead giveaway.

Did you hear about
the butcher who
backed into a
meat grinder?
He got a little
behind in his work.

Crombie Jardine
PUBLISHING LIMITED

13 Nonsuch Walk, Cheam, Surrey, SM2 7LG
www.crombiejardine.com

Published by Crombie Jardine Publishing Limited
First edition, 2006

ISBN 1-905102-66-6

Designed by www.glensaville.com
Printed and bound in Great Britain by
William Clowes Ltd, Beccles, Suffolk

THOUGHT FOR THE DAY

A PUN IS ITS OWN REWORD

Two ropes walked into a bar. The bartender said to the rope, "Hey! Sorry, but we don't serve ropes in here!" so one of the ropes left. The other rope frayed up his hair and tied himself in a knot. The bartender said to the rope, "Aren't you a rope, too?" and the rope said, "No, I'm afraid not."

CONTENTS

Which Knight

drools a lot?

Sir Liva.

Which Knight makes pottery?

Sir Amic.

Sir Lancelot once had a very

bad dream about his horse.

It was a knight mare.

FOUR WORD: WHAT IS A PUN?

A pun is a clever or witty remark, a humorous use of words that involves a word or phrase that has more than one possible meaning.

In Italian, 'puntiglio' means 'a fine point', as in a small (and usually unimportant) distinction and is most probably the source of the English word 'punctilious'.

A pun is defined by Webster as *the humorous use of a word, or of words which are formed or sounded alike but have different meanings, in such a way as to play on two or more of the possible applications; a play on words.*

Hanging is too good for a man who makes puns; he should be drawn and quoted.

Fred Allen

ALL IN
A DAY'S
WORK

Acupuncture:

A jab well done.

Bakers trade bread recipes on a
knead to know basis.

Why do bagpipers walk when they play?
They're trying to get away from the noise.

WORKING PUNS

I used to assemble new automobiles,

but then I retired.

I used to be a ballet dancer,

but found it too-too difficult.

I used to be a banker,

but lost interest in the work.

I used to be a blackjack host,

but was offered a better deal.

I used to be a butler,

but found the work wasn't my cup of tea.

I used to be a carpenter,

but then I got bored.

I used to be a hotel clerk,

but then I had reservations.

I used to be a lumberjack,

but then I got the axe.

I used to be a pimp,

but then I got laid off.

I used to be a printer,

but never made a good impression.

I used to be a tailor,

but found the work to be just so-so.

I used to be a taxi driver,

but found I couldn't hack it.

I used to be a taxidermist,

but just didn't have the right stuff.

I used to be a tennis instructor,

but it just wasn't my racket.

I used to be a transplant surgeon,

but my heart just wasn't in it.

I used to be a Velcro salesman,
but couldn't stick with it.

I used to be a Viagra salesman,
but just couldn't keep up.

I used to sell ovens,
but then I was fired.

I used to work for the Inland Revenue,

but it was just too taxing.

CAREER
OPPORTUNITIES

~

My first job was working in an orange juice
factory, but I got canned... couldn't seem to
concentrate.

Then I worked in the woods as a lumberjack,
but I just couldn't hack it, so they gave me
the axe.

After that I tried to be a tailor, but that too was
a poor fit. I guess I wasn't suited for it.

Somehow I managed to get a job working as a
pool guy, but the work was just too draining,

and I nearly went off the deep end.

Then I tried to be a cook (hoping it would add a little spice to my life) but I just didn't have the thyme to learn how to do it right.

I next worked in a deli, but any way I sliced it, I couldn't seem to cut the mustard.

My favourite job was as a backup musician, but eventually I found I wasn't noteworthy enough.

All this while I'd been studying to become a doctor. I finally started my practice but never had enough patience to make a living at it.

Next I became a professional fisherman, but discovered that I couldn't survive on my net income.

After many years of trying to find steady work

I finally got a job as a historian, but gave it up when I realized there was no future in it.

My last job was working at Starbucks. I was already getting tired of the same old grind when they fired me because I kept giving people LARGE cups when they asked for a grande.

SO I RETIRED, AND FOUND I AM PERFECT FOR THE JOB!

~

Did you hear about the butcher who

backed into a meat grinder?

He got a little behind in his work.

Archaeologist:

A man whose career lies in ruins.

PRIME SUSPECTS AT WORK

A workman was killed at a construction site. The police began questioning a number of the other workers. On account of their past brushes with the law, many of these workers were considered prime suspects.

They were a motley crew. Here is how the facts of the case shaped up:

The carpenter thought he was a stud. He had tried to frame another man one time.

The electrician was suspected of wire-tapping once but was never charged.

The glazier went to great panes to conceal his past. He still claims that he didn't do anything, and that he was framed.

The mason was a suspect because he gets stoned regularly.

The painter had a brush with the law several years ago.

The cabinet maker is an accomplished counter fitter.

The autopsy led the police to arrest the carpenter, who subsequently confessed. The evidence against him was irrefutable, because it was found that the workman, when he died, had been hammered.

The carpenter said he'd grown strong from all his dancing, but no-one believed him. It was obvious to all that he was bearing waltz fitness.

NEWS
FLASH!

NEWS FLASH!

News reports have filtered in early this morning
that US forces have swooped on an Iraqi
Primary School and detained 6th Grade teacher
Mohammed Al-Hazar. Sources indicate that,
when arrested, Al-Hazar was in possession of a
ruler, a protractor, a set square and a calculator.
US President George W Bush immediately stated
that this was clear and overwhelming evidence
that Iraq did indeed possess weapons of maths
instruction.

~

DYING IN THE PACIFIC

There were two ships crossing the Pacific. One was carrying blue paint from Singapore to Los Angeles, and the other carried red dyes from America to Taiwan. Somewhere in the middle of the ocean, the two ships met abruptly. The ships were lost to the sea and the crews of both are believed to be marooned.

At breakfast time I am so hungry
I could murder a bowl of
cornflakes. Does that make
me a cereal killer?

THE ANIMAL KINGDOM

~

What do you get when you cross a

snowman with a vampire?

Frostbite.

What has four legs, is big, green, fuzzy,

and if it fell out of a tree would kill you?

A pool table.

What is a zebra?

26 sizes larger than an "A" bra.

What lies at the bottom of the ocean and twitches?

A nervous wreck.

What is the principal part of a horse?

The mane, of course.

The trouble with skunks is that they don't have common scents.

~

Trolls are always goblin their food too quickly. Fairy-nuff, but someone should tell them it's bad for their elf.

~

I went to a seafood disco last week... and pulled a mussel.

One day at the watering hole, an elephant looked around and carefully surveyed the turtles in view.

After a few seconds' thought, he walked over to one turtle, raised his foot, and kicked the turtle as far as he could (nearly a mile).

A watching hyena asked the elephant why he had done it.

"Well, about 30 years ago I was walking through a stream and a turtle bit my foot. Finally I found the S.O.B and repaid him for what he had done to me."

"Thirty years! And you remembered... but how?!"

"I have turtle recall."

A baby pigeon was learning to fly.

But baby pigeon said, "I can't make it; I'll get too tired." His mother said, "Don't worry. I'll tie one end of a piece of string to your left leg and the other end to my right."

The baby started to cry.

"What's wrong?" said the mother.

"I don't want to be pigeon towed!"

A CHELTENHAM CHRISTMAS

Riding the favourite at Cheltenham, a jockey was well ahead of the field. Suddenly he was hit on the head by a turkey and a string of sausages.

He managed to keep control of his mount and pulled back into the lead, only to be struck by a box of Christmas crackers and a dozen mince pies as he went over the last fence.

With great skill he managed to steer the horse to the front of the field once more when, on the run in, he was struck on the head by a bottle of sherry and a Christmas pudding.

Thus distracted, he succeeded in coming only second. He immediately went to the stewards to complain that he had been seriously hampered.

FANCY DRESS

A man goes to his friend's fancy dress party with nothing but a naked girl on his back.

"So what on earth are you supposed to be?" the host asks.

"I'm a snail!" the man replies.

"What a load of rubbish!" mocks his host. "How can you be a snail when all you've got is that naked girl on your back?"

"That's not just a naked girl, mate," the man replies, "that's Michelle."

Where do you find a no legged dog?

Right where you left him.

Where do you get virgin wool from?

Ugly sheep.

Two boll weevils grew up in South Carolina. One went to Hollywood and became a famous actor. The other stayed behind in the cotton fields and never amounted to much. The second one, naturally, became known as the lesser of two weevils.

A three-legged dog walks into a
saloon in the Old West. He sidles
up to the bar and announces,
"I'm looking for the man
who shot my paw."

RUDOLPH THE RED

Rudolph the Red was sitting in his cabin in the heart of Russia eating his supper with his wife. Looking out of the window his wife remarked that it was snowing outside. "No it isn't," said Rudolph, "It's raining". His wife was convinced that she was right and so went outside to check the weather. Finding that what looked like snow was really only rain, she came back indoors and told Rudolph that he was right. "How did you know?" she asked. He replied, "Rudolph the Red knows rain, dear."

COLD LITTLE BIRD

A married man had only one complaint: his wife was always nursing sick birds. One cold February evening, he came home to find a raven with a splint on its wing sitting in his favourite chair. On the dining room table, instead of dinner, there was a feverish eagle pecking at an aspirin. In the kitchen, his wife was comforting a shivering little wren she had found half-buried in the snow.

The furious husband strode over to where his wife was drying the cold little bird with a towel. "I can't take it any more! We've got to get rid of all of these fucking birds!"

The wife held up her hand and cut him off in mid-sentence. "Please, dear, no swearing in front of the chilled wren."

THE EE

An exotic animal collector was finally
able to complete his collection with the
acquisition of a juvenile member of a very
rare species called the Ee. The animal
looked like a furry, round ball, with feet.
However, the collector knew little about
this creature, especially how much it
would grow. And it grew and grew, and it
ate and ate more and more. It grew at an
alarming rate. The small animal enclosure
had to be enlarged, and enlarged, and
enlarged again. All too soon, the size
of the creature had become alarming,
and the amount of food consumed was
straining the collector's budget. Finally, in
a state of desperation, he took the animal
in a truck to the edge of a gigantic cliff
with the idea that he would drop it over
the edge. Just as the collector was getting

set to roll the animal out of the truck, the animal popped open an eye, looked at him and asked, "What are you going to do now?" The collector explained that despite it being a very rare species he could no longer afford to keep the animal, and that dropping it over the cliff would be a humane way to get rid of such an expensive liability. The animal looked over the edge and, with a tear in its eye, sniffed, "It's a long way to tip a rare Ee."

~

When my cat lost her three male
kittens, who did she call?

Missing purr sons, of course!

Did you hear about the man
who dressed up as a baby horse?

He made a complete foal of himself.

AWOL

A sailor was caught AWOL as he tried to sneak on board his ship at about 3 a.m. The chief petty officer caught him and ordered him to stop. Upon hearing the sailor's lame explanation for his tardiness, the officer ordered, "Take this broom and sweep every link on this anchor chain by morning or it's the brig for you!

The sailor began to pick up the broom and start performing his charge. As he began to sweep, a tern landed on the broom handle. The sailor yelled at the bird to leave, but it wouldn't. The young man picked the tern off the broom handle, giving the bird a toss. The bird left, only to return and light once again on the broom handle. The sailor went through the same routine all over again, with the same result. He couldn't get any cleaning done because he could only sweep at the chain once or twice before the blasted bird returned. When morning came, so did the chief petty officer, to check up on his wayward sailor.

"What the hell have you been doing all night? This chain is no cleaner than when you started! What have you to say for yourself, sailor?" barked the chief.

"Honest, chief," came the reply, "I tossed a tern all night and couldn't sweep a link!"

READERS AND WRITERS

A hungry lion was roaming through the jungle looking for something to eat. He came across two men. One was sitting under a tree and reading a book; the other was typing away on his typewriter. The lion quickly pounced on the man reading the book and devoured him. Even the king of the jungle knows that readers digest and writers cramp.

~

~

In a small country pub, all the patrons had
become quite used to the pub owner's little dog
being around the bar, so they were quite upset
when the little dog died one day.

Everyone met to decide how they could
remember the animal. The decision was to cut
off his tail and stick it up behind the bar.

The little dog went to Heaven and was about
to run through the pearly gates when he was
stopped by Saint Peter, who questioned him as
to where he was going.

The little dog said, "I have been a good dog, so I am going into Heaven where I belong!"

Saint Peter replied, "Heaven is a place of perfection, you cannot come in without a tail. Where is your tail?"

The little dog explained what had happened back on Earth. Saint Peter told him to go back down and retrieve his tail. The little dog protested that it was now the middle of the night on Earth, but Saint Peter would not change his mind.

So the little dog went back and scratched on the door of the pub until the bartender who lived upstairs came down and opened the door.

"My goodness, it is the spirit of the little dog. What can I do for you?", he asked.

The little dog explained that he wasn't allowed into Heaven without his tail, and he needed it back.

The bartender replied, "I would really like to help you, but my license doesn't allow me to retail spirits after hours!"

HORNY DOLPHINS

The proprietor of a big aquarium was terribly
upset and called over her assistant.

"We have a bunch of school children coming
over tomorrow. I just looked in and those horny
dolphins are continuously mating. We can't let
the kids see that."

"What can we do about it?" the assistant asked.

"The only thing that will make them stop
is to feed them baby seagulls," she replied.
"You'll have to go get them, but it won't be
easy. There's a bunch of them at the city zoo.
You'll have to break in tonight, grab the little
birds and bring them back here. But be careful.
There's a stony faced old lion who guards the
birdhouse at the zoo and he'll eat you if you
make too much noise."

That night, the aquarium assistant sneaked into the zoo, quietly entered the bird house and made off with a sack full of baby seagulls. He was outside the zoo and about to head back to the office with his sack when suddenly there were policemen everywhere. Surprised at being caught, he asked an officer what was being charged with.

"Don't you know?" said the policeman, "Transporting young gulls across a staid lion for immoral porpoises!"

RUSTY

A marine biologist at the University of
New Brunswick was working on a project
that would allow humans to talk to fish,
and fish to talk to humans.

One day, after many years of working in the
lab, the system was ready for field testing.
The scientist took his gear down to a local
salmon stream and set it up. Lo and behold,
the system worked! Our hero began talking
to the salmon in the stream and the salmon
began talking back to the scientist. The scientist
noticed that one particular salmon looked a
little different from the rest. This salmon was
a darker reddish brown than the others, so he
nicknamed him Rusty.

The scientist then struck up quite a friendship with Rusty. Rusty told the scientist what it was like to be a fish, and the scientist told Rusty what it was like to be a human being.

One day, after two seasons by the stream, Rusty said, "It's time for me to leave for the ocean."

The marine biologist responded, "No, Rusty! You can't! Do you know how dangerous the trip will be? Do you know that the return rate for your species is about 2%? Do you know that there are many dangers you will have to face on the journey: fishermen, sharks and pollution to name just a few."

"Look," said Rusty, "A salmon's gotta do what a salmon's gotta do."

So off he went. Two years later, the scientist was still working by the same stream, when he heard a familiar voice from the past. Rusty had returned! The two of them quickly became reacquainted.

"You know, you were right about all the dangers!" said Rusty, "I lost track of the number of times that I was almost caught in a fisherman's net. I lost count of the number of times that I was almost eaten by sharks. But let me tell you," Rusty continued, "about the amazing sights I witnessed."

"Tell me what you saw!" said the scientist excitedly.

"The ship wrecks were incredible!" The scientist explained to Rusty about the large number of ships that were sunk in the North Atlantic.

"Well one ship I saw, the Titanic, was really fantastic! It was just amazing! I swam all through it, up the grand staircases, down into the dining salons... It was so moving that I decided to write some poetry about it."

"That must be really beautiful stuff," said the scientist.

"Oh it is. Maybe you could help me get it published?" said Rusty.

"Sure," said the scientist, "Do you have a title for your poems?"

"Yes: *Salmon Rusty's Titanic Verses!*"

FOOD
&
DIET

BEING OVERWEIGHT

IS NO WEIGH

TO LIVE.

Have you heard of the Mexican ghost named Jose?

They call him, 'No Weigh, Jose'.

I tried to make the plump ladies see the error of their weighs.

Overweight?

Remember, you earn your weigh.

RELISH TODAY.

KETCHUP TOMORROW.

WOKING IS CAUSING QUITE A STIR.

ARE YOU GOING THE WRONG WEIGH?

DIETING IS A MATTER

OF LIFE AND BREADTH.

Here is a death sentence:

IF YOU EAT LOTS OF FAT AND GREASE,

YOU WILL CEASE.

Why won't melons elope in Las Vegas?

They cantaloupe.

Did you hear about the raisin

who cheated on his wife?

It was in the newspaper, in the

current affairs section.

Once I got angry at the chef of an Italian

restaurant, so *I gave him a pizza my mind.*

A German farmer with relatives in America sent them a package consisting of some pork sausages made from his old pig. When they complained that the package had not yet arrived, he wrote: "Cheer up. The wurst is yet to come."

A boy was bagging groceries at a supermarket. One day the store installed a machine for squeezing fresh orange juice. Intrigued, the young man asked if he could be allowed to work the machine, but his request was denied. Said the store manager, "Sorry, kid, but baggers can't be juicers."

~

A mushroom walks into a bar,

sits down and orders a drink.

The bartender says,

"We don't serve mushrooms here."

The mushroom says,

"Why not? I'm a fun guy!

~

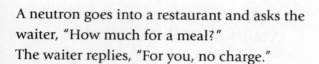

A neutron goes into a restaurant and asks the waiter, "How much for a meal?"
The waiter replies, "For you, no charge."

~

The shop assistant asked whether I wanted it measured in pounds or kilos, so I just told him that either weigh would do.

~

Did you hear about the dyslexic Satanist?

He sold his soul to Santa.

Did you hear about the guy that lost his left arm and leg in a car crash?

He's all right now.

How do crazy people go through the forest?

They take the psycho path.

~

How do you get holy water?

Boil the hell out of it.

How does a spoiled rich girl

change a light bulb?

She says, "Daddy, I want a new apartment."

What did the fish say when he

hit a concrete wall?

"Dam!"

~

What do Eskimos get from sitting

on the ice too long?

Polaroids.

What do prisoners use to call each other?

Cell phones.

What do you call a boomerang

that doesn't work?

A stick.

~

What do you call cheese that isn't yours?

Nacho cheese.

What do you call Santa's helpers?

Subordinate Clauses.

What do you call four bull fighters in quicksand?

Quatro sinko.

~

Why was the Zombie surprised
when his ghoulfiend showed up
for their date at 11p.m?

He didn't ex-spectre until midnight.

I entered a local Pun Contest. I sent in
ten different puns in the hope that at least
one of the puns would win.

Unfortunately, no pun in ten did.

~

Why can people never take a second

polygraph test?

Because they can't be re-lied upon.

What do you get from a pampered cow?

Spoiled milk.

What's the difference between roast beef

and pea soup?

Anyone can roast beef.

~

Why can't a bicycle stand alone?

Because it is two-tired.

What's the definition of a will?

A dead giveaway.

Time flies like an arrow.

Fruit flies like a banana.

A backward poet writes inverse.

In democracy it's your vote that counts;
in feudalism it's your count that votes.

She had a boyfriend with a wooden leg, but
broke it off.

A chicken crossing the road is poultry
in motion.

If you don't pay your exorcist you get
repossessed.

With her marriage she got a new name
and a dress.

Show me a piano falling down a mineshaft and
I'll show you A-flat minor.

When a clock is hungry it goes back
four seconds.

The man who fell into an upholstery machine is
fully recovered.

A grenade thrown into a kitchen in France
would result in Linoleum Blownapart.

A boiled egg in the morning is hard to beat.

He had a photographic memory which was
never developed.

A plateau is a high form of flattery.

The short fortune teller who escaped from
prison was a small medium at large.

Those who get too big for their britches will be
exposed in the end.

When you've seen one shopping centre you've seen a mall.

Those who jump off a Parisian bridge
are in Seine.

When an actress saw her first strands of grey hair she thought she'd dye.

Marathon runners with bad footwear suffer the agony of defeat.

I recently spent money on detergent to unclog my kitchen sink. It was money down the drain.

A jury is never satisfied with the verdict...
it always returns it.

I used to be twins...
My mother has a picture of me when I was two.

What is the difference between a conductor
and a teacher?
*The conductor minds the train and a teacher
trains the mind.*

Two ferocious cannibal chiefs sat licking their
fingers after a large meal.

"Your wife makes a delicious roast," one
chief said.

"Thanks," his friend said, "I'm gonna miss her."

Hangover:

The wrath of grapes.

Income Tax:

Capital punishment.

~

A used car is not always

what it's jacked up to be.

Two silkworms were in a race.

They ended up in a tie.

~

~

To my sweetheart:

My cooking's gotten better since I fondue.

Egotist:

One who is me-deep in conversation.

~

~

Did you hear about the Buddhist who refused
his dentist's Novocain during root canal work?

He wanted to transcend dental medication.

Did you hear about the woman who started
dating rakes?

She fell on hard tines.

~

~

Kleptomaniac:

One who can't help himself from helping himself.

~

California smog test:

Can UCLA?

LIFE'S LITTLE IMPUNDERABLES

Dijon vu: the same mustard as before?

Can you fire a masseuse for rubbing you up the wrong way?

Was banning the bra a big flop?

Is an Englishman's home is his castle, in a manor of speaking?

Why is a pessimist's blood type always B-negative?

Is my wife just making pottery to kiln time?

When the Energizer Bunny was arrested was he really charged with battery?

Is a Freudian slip when you say one thing but mean your mother?

Is a successful diet the triumph of mind over platter?

Does a man really need a mistress just to break the monogamy?

Is marriage the mourning after the knot before?

Is a book on voyeurism a peeping tome?

Is dancing cheek-to-cheek really a form of floor play?

When you dream in colour, is it a pigment of your imagination?

Are cardboard belts just a waist of paper?

Does the name Pavlov ring a bell?

Shotgun wedding: a case of wife or death?

Is a gossip simply someone with a great
sense of rumour?

Without geometry, would life be pointless?

A hangover: the wrath of grapes?

Should condoms be used on every
conceivable occasion?

Does reading whilst sunbathing make
you well-red?

When two egotists meet, is it an I for an I?

A thief broke into the local police station and stole all the lavatory equipment.

A spokesperson was quoted as saying, "We have absolutely nothing to go on."

A woman had twins and gave them up for adoption. One of them went to live with a family in Egypt, and was named Amal. The other went to a family in Spain who named him Juan.

Years later, Juan sent a photo of himself to his birth mother. Upon receiving the photo, she told her husband that she would really love a photo of Amal too.

Her husband responded, "But they are twins! If you've seen Juan, you've seen Amal."

Just as a surgeon was finishing up an operation the patient woke up, sat up and demanded to know what was going on.

"I'm about to close," the surgeon said. The patient then grabbed his hand, saying, "Oh, no you're not! I'll close my own incision."

The doctor handed him the needle and said, "Suture self."

~

At Scotland's Glasgow University, the following note was seen hanging on a lecturer's door:

Today's tutorial is cancelled because Dr. N. is il [sic].

~

A new nurse listened while Dr. Slater
yelled, "Typhoid! Tetanus! Measles!"

The new nurse asked another nurse, "Why
is he doing that?"

The other nurse replied, "Oh, he just likes
to call the shots around here."

~

A pregnant woman from Oklahoma has a car accident which results in her being in a coma. Upon waking, she sees she's no longer pregnant and she asks the doctor about her baby.

The doctor smiles and replies, "Ma'am you've had twins, a boy and a girl. Your brother from Arkansas came in and named them."

The woman thinks to herself, "God, why did it have to be my brother... he's an idiot!"

She asks him, "Well, what's the girl's name?"
"Denise."
"Wow, that's not a bad name, I like it! What's the boy's name?"
"Denephew."

An official stopped a man in the hospital
car park.
"You can't park here. It's badge holders only."
"But I have got a bad shoulder!" he replied.

The Mexican doctor told the village
nymphomaniac, "Senorita, it looks to me like
you've had Juan too many."

A man rushed into the doctor's office and
shouted, "Doctor! I think I'm shrinking!"
The doctor calmly responded, "Now, settle
down. You'll just have to be a little patient."

MEDICAL DICTIONARY

ALIMENTARY: What Sherlock Holmes said to Dr. Watson.

ANALLY: Occurring yearly.

ANTIBODY: Against everyone.

ARTERY: The study of fine paintings.

ATTENUATE: What Bo Derek says to less attractive women.

BACTERIA: The back door to a cafeteria.

BANDAGES: The Rolling Stones.

BENIGN: What we want when we are eight.

BOTULISM: The tendency to make mistakes.

BOWEL: Letters like A, E, I, O, or U.

CAESAREAN SECTION: A district in Rome.

CARDIOLOGY: The advanced study of poker playing.

CARPAL: Someone you drive to work with.

CASTRATE: The going price for setting a fracture.

CAT SCAN: Searching for one's lost kitty.

CAUTERIZE: What the med student did before he winked at his date.

COLIC: A sheep dog.

COMA: A punctuation mark.

CONGENITAL: Friendly.

CONSTIPATION: Endangered faeces.

CORTIZONE: The local courthouse.

DENIAL: Where Cleopatra used to swim.

DILATE: To live long.

ELIXIR: What a dog does to his owner when she gives him a bone.

ENEMA: Opposite of a friend.

ENTERITIS: A penchant for burglary.

FESTER: Quicker.

FIBRILLATE: To tell a small lie.

FIBULA: A small lie.

GENES: Blue denim trousers.

GRIPPE: What you do to a suitcase.

HANGNAIL: A coat hook.

HEMORRHOID: A male from outer space.

HERNIA: Pertaining to a female's knee.

HERPES: What women do in the Ladies Room.

HORMONES: What a prostitute does when she doesn't get paid.

HUMERUS: To tell us what we want to hear.

IMPOTENT: Distinguished, well known.

INBRED: The best way to have your jam.

INPATIENT: Tired of waiting.

INTESTINE: Currently taking an exam.

LABOUR PAIN: Hurt at work.

MEDICAL STAFF: A doctor's cane.

MORBID: A higher offer.

NITRATE: Lower than day rate.

NODE: Was aware of.

ORGANIC: Church musician.

OUTPATIENT: A person who has fainted.

PARADOX: Two doctors.

PARALYZE: Two far-fetched stories.

PATHOLOGICAL: A reasonable way to go.

PELVIS: A cousin of Elvis.

PENIS: Someone who plays the piano.

PHARMACIST: A person who makes a living dealing in agriculture.

PLASTER CAST: The drunk roadies backstage at a rock concert.

PROSTATE: Flat on your back.

PROTEIN: In favour of young people.

RECOVERY ROOM: A place to upholster furniture.

RECTUM: Damn near killed him.

RED BLOOD COUNT: Dracula.

RHEUMATIC: Amorous.

SACRUM: Holy.

SCAR: Rolled tobacco leaf.

SECRETION: Hiding something.

SEIZURE: Roman Emperor.

SPERM: To reject, look away from.

STERILE SOLUTION: Not using the elevator during a fire.

SURGERY: A reason to get an uninterruptible power supply.

TABLET: A small table.

TERMINAL ILLNESS: Getting sick at the airport.

TESTES: What you order when you don't know what the patient has.

TIBIA: A country in North Africa.

TOLERANCE: What you get if you give growth hormone to ants.

TUMOR: An extra pair.

URINATE: What a nurse would say if a patient asked her what room he's in.

URINE: The opposite of "You're out!"

VARICOSE: Very near.

VEIN: Conceited.

VERTIGO: How foreigners ask for directions.

WHITE COUNT: The number of Caucasians.

~

TRANSPORT

If you step onto a plane and recognize a friend of yours named Jack don't yell out, "Hi Jack!"

The astronauts said their experience on the moon was out of this world but that the cost of the space programme was astronomical.

Travelling on a flying carpet is a rugged experience.

An astronaut broke the law of gravity and got a suspended sentence.

ON THE ROAD TO NOWHERE

A Motorway and a Dual Carriageway are in a really rough pub enjoying a burly pint of cloudy scrumpy to demonstrate just how hard they are.

The Dual Carriageway is impressing a few pretty little A-roads with his central reservation whilst the Motorway is showing off about his hard shoulder and they're all getting on really well.

The two are just about to take the A-Roads 'back to their place' when a piece of Pink Tarmac comes through the door. The Motorway and the Dual Carriageway turn white with fear and dive for cover under the table.

The A-Roads (having thought the Motorway and Dual Carriageway were hard) are not impressed by this behaviour. The Pink Tarmac downs a triple vodka and walks out of the bar. The Motorway and Dual Carriageway get out from under the table, realizing that they've blown it with the A-Roads.

The first A-Road asks the Motorway, "Why did you go white and dive for cover when that pink piece of tarmac walked in? You're supposed to be the king of the roads!"

The Motorway replies, "Why?! That guy's a fucking Cycle Path, that's why!!"

ACROSS THE POND

~

Two Eskimos sitting in a kayak were chilly, but when they lit a fire in the craft, it sank… proving once and for all that you can't have your kayak and heat it, too.

~

A botanist had just returned from an expedition to the South Pacific Islands and was discussing his adventures with his colleagues back at the university where he taught.

"What was the most exciting discovery you found there?" asked a fellow professor.

He replied, "The people native to this one island had discovered the most amazing cure for constipation. Using only the leafs of the local palm trees they concocted a suppository which quickly cured the ailment."

Another professor asked, "A palm leaf suppository? Did it really work?"

Replied the botanist, "With fronds like these... who needs enemas."

~

Back in the 1800s, the Tates Watch Company of Massachusetts wanted to produce other products and, since they already made the cases for pocket watches, decided to market compasses for the pioneers travelling west.

It turned out that although their watches were of finest quality, their compasses were so bad that people often ended up in Canada or Mexico rather than California.

This, of course, is the origin of the expression:

He who has a Tates is lost!

~

A famous Viking explorer returned home from a voyage and found his name missing from the town register. His wife insisted on complaining to the local civic official who apologized profusely saying, "I must have taken Leif off my census."

~

BIG CHESS TOURNAMENT

The big chess tournament was taking place
at the Plaza in New York. After the first
day's competition, many of the winners
were sitting around in the foyer of the hotel
talking about their matches and bragging
about their wonderful play. After a few drinks
they started getting louder and louder until
finally, the desk clerk couldn't take any more
and kicked them out.

The next morning the Manager called the clerk
into his office and told him there had been
many complaints about his being so rude to the
hotel guests... instead of kicking them out, he
should have just asked them to be less noisy.
The clerk responded, "I'm sorry, but if there's
one thing I can't stand, it's chess nuts boasting
in an open foyer."

The first attempt to build the Channel Tunnel was started in France in the 1890s. It would have been the longest steam train tunnel in the world, but they stopped when they realised they'd Britain off more than they could choo.

~

My wife's gone to the West Indies

Jamaica?

No, she went of her own accord.

My wife's gone to the Indian coast.

Goa?

Phwoar! I'll say!

My wife's gone to St Petersburg.

Is she Russian?

No, she's taking her time.

My wife's gone to Northern Italy

Genoa?

I should think so, we've been married
for 20 years.

My wife's gone to the Welsh border.

Wye?

Search me.

My wife's gone to the botanical gardens.

Kew?

Yes, it was rather busy.

My wife's gone to Malawi.

Lilongwe?

Yes, about 5000 miles.

My wife's gone on a singing tour of South Korea.

Seoul?

No, R&B.

My wife smoked a joint near Manchester.

In Hale?

Yep, got absolutely wasted.

ART ATTACK

Recently a man in Paris nearly got away with stealing several paintings from the Louvre.

However, after planning the crime, and getting in and out past security, he was captured only two blocks away when his Econoline ran out of gas.

When asked how he could mastermind such a crime and then make such an obvious error, he replied:

"I had no Monet to buy Degas to make the Van Gogh."

At one time, economic conditions caused the closing of several small clothing mills in the English countryside. A man from West Germany bought the buildings and converted them into dog kennels for the convenience of German tourists who liked to have their pets with them while vacationing in England. One summer evening, a local resident called to his wife to come out of the house.

"Just listen!", he urged. "The Mills Are Alive With the Hounds of Munich!"

A TRIBE WITHIN AFRICA

There was a tribe in Africa which was very fierce and warring... they would do battle with all the tribes in the area, and they always won. As a victory trophy, they would take the throne of the chief of the defeated tribe and carry it home, chanting victory chants and singing the whole way. When they got home, they would put the throne in the attic of the grass hut. This went on for quite some time, and soon the throne collection grew, adding to the prestige of the tribe.

One day, they fought a battle with a tribe of fairly large people, some might call them giants. They won, and they struggled to get the throne home...but the chanting and joyousness prevailed as usual. When they got home, they had the ritual of putting the throne in the attic of the grass hut, but the weight was too much. The ceiling collapsed, killing everyone in the tribe.

The moral:

People who live in grass houses shouldn't stow thrones.

COLUMBUS

We all know that Columbus believed the world was round when others believed that it was flat and that if you travelled far enough you would go over the edge.

We also know that Columbus reached what we now know as America. While there are still a few people who believe that when Columbus returned to Spain he told Queen Isabella that he had discovered a new world, most people believe he told her he had reached India. Recently, documents written by Queen Isabella's official scribe were uncovered revealing what Columbus actually said on returning from his first voyage. His first words were, "I'll bet I'm the first man who ever got nineteen hundred miles on a galleon."

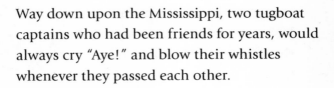

Way down upon the Mississippi, two tugboat captains who had been friends for years, would always cry "Aye!" and blow their whistles whenever they passed each other.

A new crewman asked his boat's mate, "What do they do that for?"

The mate looked surprised and replied, "You mean that you've never heard of an aye for an aye and a toot for a toot?"

A FAIR TALE

Snow White received a camera as a gift. She happily took pictures of the Dwarfs and their surroundings. When she finished her first batch she took the film to be developed. After a week or so she went to get the finished photos. The clerk said the photos were not back from the processor.

Needless to say, she was disappointed and started to cry. The clerk, trying to console her, said,

"Don't worry. Some day your prints will come".

DOUBLE
TALK
DEFINITIONS

ALARMS: What an octopus is.

ALIMONY: The bounty of mutiny.

ARCHEOLOGIST: A man whose career lies in ruins.

ATHEIST: A person with no invisible means of support.

CRICK: The sound that a Japanese camera makes.

DIPLOMACY: Lying in state.

DIPLOMAT: One who is disarming, even if his country isn't.

FLATTERY: Phony express.

INCOME TAX: Capital punishment.

PASTEURIZE:
Too far to see.

KHAKIS: What you need to start the car in Boston.

MIDDLE AGE: When actions creak louder than words.

OLYMPIC OFFICIALS: The souls that time men's tries.

PROPAGANDA: A gentlemanly goose.

PSYCHOLOGIST: A person that pulls habits out of rats.

SAXOPHONE: An ill wind nobody blows good.

A History of Boys' Boarding Schools
by
Ben Dover

A History of Bullfighting
by
Matt Adore

A Life of Crime
by
Upton O. Goode

A Step by Step Guide to French Fries
by
P. L. Potatoes

A Stitch in Time
by
Pat Chupp

Accused
by
Watts E. Dunn

All By Myself
by
Saul E. Terry

Allergies
by
P. Nutt

Alone at Sea
by
Marie Celeste

An Ill Wind
by
Isadora Jarr

An Unexpected Surprise
by
Oliver Sudden

Annual Returns
by
Abbi Birthday

Architectural Styles
by
Eddy Fiss

Asking Forgiveness
by
Neil Down

Birds
by
C. Gull

Blissful Days
by
Trudy Light

Blood and Gore in the Black Forest
by
Horace Tory

Can't Catch Me!
by
J. L. Breaker

Carpet Fitting for Beginners
by
Walter Wall

Chinese Revenge Tactics
by
Hoo Flung Dung

Come On In!
by
Doris Open

Comic Manoeuvres
by
Stan Dupp

Computer Programming for Beginners
by
I. B. Emm

Cooking with Clementine
by
Omar Darling

Cooking with Eggs
by
Sue Flay

Criminal Casebook
by
Kermit A. Krime

Crying Wolf
by
Al Armist

Daily Exercise Regimes
by
Y. B. Phatt

Dental Nightmares
by
Phil Mcavity

Dieting Made Simple
by
Ann O'Rexic

Dieting Tips
by
Will Power

Disaster
by
Kat A Stroffey

Dog Training
by
Kay Nine

Don't Ask Me Why
by
Howard I. Know

Drunk and Disorderly Conduct
by
Honour Bender

Dull Thudding Pain
by
A. King

Embarrassing Medical Conditions
by
Ivan Itch

Embarrassing Moments
by
Lucy Lastik

Empty Plates
by
Arthur Anymore

Everything's Passing Me By
by
Buster Tyre

Explosives Made Easy
by
Stan Wellback

Fading Away
by
Peter Out

Faking It
by
Count R. Fitz

Falling
by
Eileen Doubt

Farting for Britain
by
Hugh Jass

Felling Trees
by
Tim Burr

Forgive and Forget
by
Stan Byerman

Fractions for Fun
by
Lois C. Denominator

Friday 13th
by
Paul Bearer

Fun For One
by
Master Bates

Getting Old is When...
by
I.P. Nightly

Give it all You've Got!
by
Eve Ho

Grammatical Errors of Today
by
Miss Takes

Grave Times
by
Paul Bearer

Greenhouse Tips
by
Tom Mato

He Didn't Make It
by
D. O. Way

Hide and Seek
by
I. C. Hugh

Hot or Cold?
by
Luke Warm

House Construction Made Easy
by
Bill Jerome Holme

How to Diet
by
F. V. Load

How to Get Ahead in Advertising
by
Bill Board

How to Look Younger in Seven Days
by
Fay Slift

Hypnotic Moments
by
N. Tranced

I Knew You Would Say That
by
Claire Voyant

I Say It As I See It
by
Frank O. Pinion

I Tried
by
Noah Veil

If at First you Don't Succeed...
by
Percy Vere

Into the Void
by
M. T. Ness

It Happens for a Reason
by
K. Sarah Cerra

It Wasn't Me!
by
Ivan Alibi

It's in his Kiss
by
Miss L. Toe

Italian Cuisine, Vol 1
by
Ravi Oley

Italian Cuisine, Vol 2
by
Minnie Stroni

Italian Cuisine, Vol 3
by
Lynn Guini

Keeping Secrets
by
Kent Tellem

Let me Help You
by
Abel N. Willin

Life's a Bitch
by
Y. Me

Lighting for Special Occasions
by
Sean D'Olier

Loopholes of the Law
by
Ellie Gull

Macho Men
by
Seymore Hair

Masterpieces
by
Art Tistic

Me, Me, Me
by
Frank Lee Boring

Men Getting Lost
by
Reed Demapp

Mental Health Issues
by
Cy Kosis

Money Management for the Desperate
by
Owen Cash

Motoring Made Easy
by
Rhonda Bout

Never
by
Kurt Reply

Never Borrow Money
by
Nora Lender Bee

New Year's Resolutions
by
Jan U. Arie

Nicely Turned Out
by
Preston Ironed

No Crystal Balls
by
Reid Palms

On the Old MacDonald Farm
by
E. I. Eeyioh

One-Armed Bandit Territory
by
R. Kade

Optical Illusions
by
Seymour Clearly

Overcoming Shyness
by
Greg Garious

Overwhelming Sadness
by
Mel. N. Collie

Pasta King
by
Al Dente

Peace on Earth
by
Olive Branch

Peckham
by
Helen Earth

Plain Untruths
by
Liza Little

Plumbing for Beginners
by
Lee K. Fawcette

Pre-Millennium Dome
by
Robin Banks

Publishing in the 21st Century
by
Maggie Zeene

Putdown Lines
by
F. U. Two

Pygmies of West Africa
by
R. U. Short

Quick and Easy
by
T. V. Dinner

Robots
by
Anne Droid

Running to Catch the 4:50 Train
by
Willy Makeit

Scary Mary
by
Emma Fraid

Shocking Tales
by
Alec Tricity

Snow Drifts
by
Ava Lanche

So Far So Good
by
Chester Field

Straight Road Ahead
by
Laurie Driver

Suspense Writing
by
Toby Continued

Tarzan Tales
by
C. Dick & Jane Run

Teetotalling Tales
by
Mustafa Drink

The Art Of Falling In Love
by
Q. Pidd

The Bad Week
by
Gladys Friday

The Beatles' Greatest Hits
by
Tristan Shout

The Blushing Bride
by
Rosie Cheeks

The Disappearing Daughter
by
Fay Daway

The Fascination of the Female
by
Norma Stitz

The Full English Monty
by
Chris P. Bacon and Ann Negg

The Gossip Girls
by
Phyllis Zinn

The Gullible Warden
by
Freida Convict

The Hitchhiker's Dream
by
Juan Nalift

The Insomniac
by
Eliza Wake

The Joy of Cylindrical Filing
by
Chuck Kitt

The Life and Times of Ian Fleming
by
J. M. Spond

The Long Walk Home
by
Miss Debus

The Misery of Migraines
by
Ivan Hedake

The Mis-management of Money
by
I. O. Lots

The Mysteries of the Male Anatomy
by
Hugh G. Rection

The Need for Insurance
by
Justin Case

The Need to Take It Easy
by
Ed. G. Nerfs

The Pros of Synthetic Fabrics
by
Polly Ester

The Search for Britian's Fastest Athelete
by
C. Howie Runns

The Way to Bethlehem
by
Dusty Rhodes

The White Cliffs of Dover
by
Vera Way

The Young Lion Tamer
by
Claude Bottom

Top of the Class
by
B. D. Best

Toys of Yesteryear
by
Ted E. Behr

Traditional Nursey Rhymes
by
Barbara Blacksheep

Travelling Lightly
by
C. D. World

Troublesome Neighbours
by
Lotta Noyze

Underwear Essentials
by
Nick R. Elastic

Unsolved Mysteries
by
Ima Crook

Victorian Times
by
Orson Buggy

What have We Here?
by
Lauren Order

What I Really, Really Want
by
Trudy Zire

Will Writing for Professionals
by
Ben E. Factor

Willing You On
by
Benny Fishery

Words
by
Dick Shunnary

~

~

An author did all his writing from a study beneath his house. It was a very cryptic book, but it was at a bargain-basement price, so he ended up with a best cellar.

~

A bun is the lowest form of wheat.

Anon

A man who could make so vile a pun

would not scruple to pick a pocket.

John Dennis

Hanging is too good for a man who makes

puns; he should be drawn and quoted.

Fred Allen

He that would pun, would pick a pocket.

Alexander Pope

The eleventh pun always gets a laugh,
even if no pun in ten did.

Anon

The pun is mightier than the sword.

James Joyce

The World's Funniest Proverbs

JAMES ALEXANDER

Beauty is in the eye of the beer holder.

Don't take life too seriously – it's not permanent.

Multi-tasking: the art of screwing up everything all at once.

Never marry for money; you will borrow cheaper

1-905102-02-X • £3.99

The World's Funniest Laws

JAMES ALEXANDER

In Arizona you can go to prison for 25 years for cutting down a cactus!

Do not say "oh boy" in Jonesborough, Georgia. It's illegal!

On Sundays in Florida, widows must not go parachuting!

It is against the law to take a lion to the cinema in Baltimore!

1-905102-10-0 • £4.99

If you have any comments or

suggestions about this book, please

email puns@crombiejardine.com.

www.crombiejardine.com